# Energy Essentials

# Renewable Energy

EXPRESS EDITION

Nigel Saunders and Steven Chapman

Raintree

For information, address the publisher:
Raintree, 100 N. LaSalle, Suite 1200, Chicago, IL 60602

Printed and bound in China
10 09 08 07 06
10 9 8 7 6 5 4 3 2 1

**Library of Congress Cataloging-in-Publication Data**

Saunders, N. (Nigel)
    Renewable energy / Nigel Saunders and Steven Chapman.
        p. cm. -- (Energy essentials)
    Includes bibliographical references and index.
    ISBN 1-4109-1696-0 (library binding-hardcover) --
    ISBN 1-4109-1701-0 (pbk.)   1.  Renewable energy sources--
Juvenile literature.   I. Chapman, Steven. II. Title.
III. Series: Saunders, N.  (Nigel).  Energy essentials.
TJ808.2.S28 2005
333.79'4--dc22
                                                    2005003831

This leveled text is a version of Freestyle: Energy Essentials: Renewable Energy.

**Acknowledgments**
p.4/5, Science Photo Library/David Hay Jones; p.4, Science Photo Library; p.5, (top) Corbis, p.5, (mid) Science Photo Library/Sinclair Stammers, (bottom) Rex Features; p.6, Alamy Images; p.6, (bottom) Science Photo Library/ Kenneth W. Fink; p.7, Photodisc; p.8/9, Rex Features; p.8, Corbis; p.9, Getty Images; pp.10/11, Corbis; p.10, Getty Images; p.11, Science Photo Library; p.12, (top) Corbis; p.12 (bottom) Science Photo Library; p.13 Science Photo Library; p.14 (top) Corbis; p.14 (bottom) Photodisc; p.15, Corbis; p.16, (top) Corbis; p.16, (bottom) Science Photo Library; p.17, Corbis; p.18 (top) Science Photo Library; p.18 (bottom) Corbis; p.19, Rex Features; p.20, Images/Imagebank; p.21 Photodisc (top, mid and bottom); pp.22/23, Science Photo Library/Alexis Rosenfeld; p.23, Alamy Images; pp.24/25 Getty Images/Imagebank; p.24 Oxford Scientific Films; p.25, Science photo Library/Burlington Electric Department/NREL/US Department of Energy; pp.26/27, Ecoscene; p.26, Corbis; p.27, Science Photo Library/Prof. David Hall; p.28 (top) Corbis; p.28 (bottom) Rex Features; p.29, Action Plus; pp. 30/31, Photodisc; p.30 and 31, Science Photo Library; p.32 (top and bottom) Science Photo Library/Martin Bond; p.33, Science Photo Library/Martin Bond; p.34 (top and bottom) Corbis; p.35, Corbis/ Hubert Stadler; pp.36/37, Oxford Scientific Films; p.36, The Photolibrary Wales; p.37, Science Photo Library/Bernard Edmaier; p.38, Science Photo Library/Martin Bond; p.39, Rex Features; p.40 (right) Corbis; p.40 (left) Science Photo Library; p.41, Science Photo Library/Martin Bond; p.42, Science Photo Library/Colin Cuthbert; p.43, Science photo Library/Chris Knapton; pp.44/45, Science Photo Library.

Cover photograph of solar panels reproduced with permission of Robert Harding Picture Library

Every effort has been made to contact copyright holders of any material reproduced in this book. Any omissions will be rectified in subsequent printings if notice is given to the publishers.

**Disclaimer:**
All the Internet addresses (URLs) given in this book were valid at the time of going to press. However, due to the dynamic nature of the Internet, some addresses may have changed, or sites may have changed or ceased to exist since publication. While the author and Publishers regret any inconvenience this may cause readers, no responsibility for any such changes can be accepted by either the author or the Publishers.

# Contents

Any words appearing in the text in bold, **like this**, are explained in the Glossary. You can also look for them in the Word Store at the bottom of each page.

# What Is Energy?

**James Joule**

Energy is measured in units called joules. One joule (J) is enough energy to run a light bulb for one sixtieth of a second. The joule is named after the British scientist James Joule (above).

**Energy** is being able to do work. It is energy that lets you to get up in the morning, get dressed, and walk to school.

Energy comes in many forms. The Sun gives out heat and light energy. A car has chemical energy stored in its fuel. Movement energy in the wind is what makes windmills turn.

▲ **Hydroelectric** power stations use the energy in moving water to make electricity.

**Word Store**   energy   being able to do work. Light, heat, and electricity are types of energy.

## Energy resources

Anything that stores or gives us energy is called an **energy resource**. **Fossil fuels** such as coal, oil, and natural gas store energy. When they are burned in **power stations**, this energy is changed into electrical energy.

Fossil fuels are being used up very quickly. When they are finished, they will be gone forever. They are **nonrenewable** energy resources. This book is about forms of energy that will not run out. These are called **renewable** energy resources.

### Find out later ...

. . . how food can be cooked for free using **solar** power.

. . . where the energy needed by living things comes from.

. . . how we can use energy from the Moon without going there.

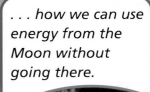

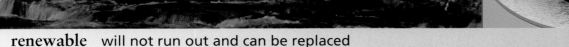

# Nonrenewable Energy

The main **nonrenewable energy resources** are coal, oil, and natural gas. These are called **fossil fuels**. They are made of the **fossilized** remains of living things that died millions of years ago.

## Coal formation

About 300 million years ago, huge, swampy forests covered a lot of Earth. When the trees died, the swamp stopped them from rotting away. Thick layers of dead plants built up and were buried by mud and sand. Over millions of years, these trees were slowly turned into coal.

### Burning carbon

Coal is made of carbon. Carbon gives out a lot of energy when it burns. Coal makes one-third of the world's electricity. But there is only enough coal left to last another 400 years.

▼ Coal was made from trees that grew in swampy places like this.

***Word store***   nonrenewable   something that will run out one day and cannot be replaced

## Oil and natural gas

Oil and natural gas were made from the bodies of tiny sea creatures that died more than 100 million years ago. When the creatures died, they sank to the bottom of the sea. The creatures were slowly covered with layers of mud and sand. Over many years, they were turned into oil and gas. The mud and sand then turned into rock, trapping them underground.

Oil is mainly used for running things such as cars and airplanes. There is probably only enough oil left in the world to last another 40 years.

### Drilling for oil

Oil companies have to drill through rock to reach trapped oil and gas. The oil rig below is pumping oil from the North Sea.

fossil fuel    fuel made from the remains of fossilized plants or animals

## Running out

We know that **fossil fuels** will run out one day. But there are some things we can do to make them last longer.

## Cost goes up

When things start to run out, they cost more. As the price of coal, oil, and natural gas goes up, people will go further and dig deeper to find them. Coal mines and oilfields that are too expensive to use at the moment will become worth opening up. This will keep fossil fuels going for a little bit longer.

**Alaskan oil**
The Trans-Alaska Oil Pipeline (above) carries oil from Alaska. It carries enough oil to supply the United States with almost one-fifth of its oil.

▶ When there is a worldwide shortage of oil, people have to line up to get a container of gasoline.

## Energy efficient

We need to make fossil fuels last longer. We can do this by using them more slowly. Modern cars are made to use less fuel and make less **pollution**. New **power stations** are also more **efficient** and use less fuel to make the same amount of electricity. Anything that wastes electricity also wastes fuel.

### Saving light

**Energy**-saving light bulbs (left) use less electricity than ordinary light bulbs — they give out less energy as wasted heat. They also last longer.

efficient   good at doing a job without wasting energy

## Pollution

When **fossil fuels** are burned, they release dangerous gases into the air. This harms the **environment** in many different ways. Two of these dangerous gases are sulfur dioxide and carbon dioxide.

## Acid rain

Sulfur dioxide mixes with **water vapor** in the air to make weak sulfuric acid. This falls to the ground in the rain. It is called **acid rain**. Acid rain damages buildings, kills trees and plants, and harms living things in rivers and lakes.

### Dying forests

These trees in the Czech Republic (below) have been killed by acid rain. Acid rain washes away important **minerals** in the soil before the trees can use them.

mineral    substance needed by plants and animals to keep them healthy

## The greenhouse effect

Some of the gases in the **atmosphere** trap the heat **energy** from the Sun. This keeps Earth warm, in the same way glass in a greenhouse keeps plants warm. This is called the **greenhouse effect**.

Carbon dioxide is a greenhouse gas. The amount of carbon dioxide in the atmosphere has increased in the last 300 years. During this time, the temperature on Earth has also risen. This process is called **global warming**. As global warming increases, the weather around the world will change.

### Heating up

The map above shows how much hotter winters in the northern hemisphere would be if the amount of carbon dioxide in the atmosphere doubled. The red areas are about 50°F (10°C) hotter than they are now.

◀ This street in Mexico City is full of traffic during the morning rush hour. Gases from the vehicles' engines cause a thick, harmful **smog**.

## Renewable energy resources

We need to stop using so many **nonrenewable energy resources**. Fortunately, there are several types of **renewable energy** resources that we can use instead.

There are five main renewable energy resources. They are:
- Light from the Sun;
- Heat from the Sun;
- **Chemical energy** stored in living things;
- Energy in moving air;
- Energy in moving water.

### Early windmills

Windmills make use of the **kinetic energy** in the wind. This Dutch windmill (above) was used for pumping water.

▶ This **solar** furnace in France uses 9,500 mirrors to **focus** the Sun's heat on to the tower on the right. Electricity can be generated from this heat.

## Benefits of renewable energy resources

- They can be found all over the world.
- They make little **pollution** and **running costs** are low.
- Using renewable energy resources means that oil can be used to make plastics and other useful things.
- They will never run out.

## Problems with renewable energy resources

- They are not always reliable. You can only get electricity from a wind farm on a windy day. You cannot get energy from the Sun at night.
- Some of the equipment needed is very expensive.

### Wind farms

The windmills on **wind farms** change the kinetic energy in the wind into electrical energy. This wind farm in California (below) provides enough electricity to run 100,000 homes.

# Energy from the Sun

The Sun is a huge ball of hot gases. The Sun releases huge amounts of **energy** as heat and light. Without this heat and light energy, our planet would be freezing cold and nothing could live on it.

The Sun is an enormous **energy resource**. The sunlight falling on the United States in one day has more than twice the energy it uses in a year. But how can we trap and use this energy?

### Powerful Sun

The amount of energy released by the Sun (right) is a hundred thousand billion times more than the largest coal-fired power station in Europe (above).

## Trapping heat

Buildings often become hot on a sunny day through a process called **passive solar** heating. The Sun warms up a building through the roof, walls, and windows. No extra help is needed to warm the house.

Buildings that face the Sun at noon will trap a lot of solar heat. Even more heat can be trapped if the walls are painted black. This is because black surfaces are very good at **absorbing** heat energy.

### Reflecting heat

In hot parts of the world, people do not want the Sun to warm up their houses too much. So they paint their buildings white (below). Light colors reflect heat energy and help keep houses cooler.

absorb   take in

## Hot water from the Sun

Where there is a lot of sunshine, you can heat water using **solar energy**. This is done by fitting a box called a solar collector to the roof of a house.

The solar collector has three layers. The first is a see-through layer that lets in the Sun's rays. The bottom layer is painted black to **absorb** as much heat as possible. In between these two layers are pipes filled with water. The water is warmed by the heat from the Sun.

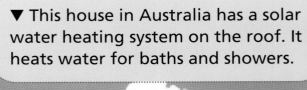
▼ This house in Australia has a solar water heating system on the roof. It heats water for baths and showers.

### Solar ovens

This is a solar oven in Kenya (below). The shiny sheets **reflect** the Sun's rays into the oven where the heat cooks the food.

## Electricity from the Sun

You can also use the Sun's heat energy to generate electricity. At solar **power stations**, a large number of mirrors **focus** the Sun's rays onto water pipes. The mirrors can move, and they follow the Sun's path across the sky.

The heat energy from the Sun is used to boil water. This makes steam that then turns a **generator**, which makes electricity.

### Solar mirrors

This man (left) is checking the mirrors at a solar power station in the Mojave Desert, in California.

focus    concentrate onto one spot

## Using the Sun's light energy

The light **energy** that comes from the Sun can be turned into electricity using **solar** cells. Some calculators have a small solar cell on the front. Larger solar cells can **absorb** enough light energy to run much bigger machines.

## Using solar cells

Solar cells are also useful in places that have no electricity supply. In some places, solar cells run traffic signals and work public telephones. Solar cells are also particularly useful in space, where it is impossible to get electricity.

### A solar cell

This is a solar cell. It is made from the same types of materials used to make computer chips.

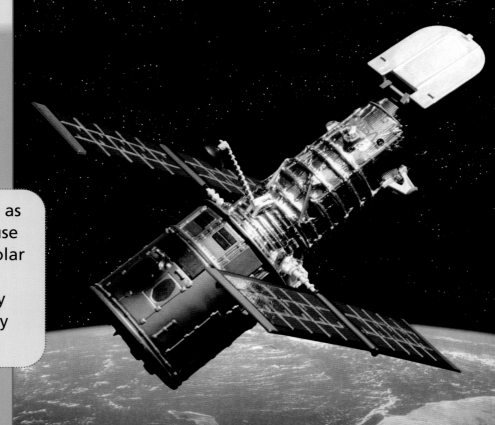

▶ **Satellites**, such as this one (right), use large panels of solar cells to turn the Sun's light energy into the electricity they need.

satellite   something that goes around a planet

## Benefits of solar energy

- Using energy from the Sun does not cause **pollution**.
- Solar energy is free.
- Solar energy will never run out.
- Using solar energy means that **fossil fuels** can be saved.

## Problems of solar energy

- You cannot get solar energy at night, and there is less of it on cloudy days.
- Solar equipment costs a lot of money.
- Expensive batteries are needed to store the electricity made during the day so it can be used at night.
- Solar cells are not very **efficient**.

### Solar-powered cars

This is an experimental solar-powered car (below). It is covered with solar cells. Solar cars produce no pollution, unlike those powered by fossil fuels. They are also cheaper to run.

# Biomass Energy

**Biomass energy** comes from energy stored in living plants. When the plants are burned, they release energy that we can then use to make electricity.

## Photosynthesis

Green plants need sunlight to grow. Their green leaves use the energy in sunlight and the gas carbon dioxide and turn them into sugars. The plants use the energy in the sugars to grow. This process is called **photosynthesis**.

### Toward the light

Because green plants need the energy from sunlight to grow, seeds will always seek out the light. If you grow some seedlings in a dark box with a light source at one side (right), the seedlings will turn toward the light.

photosynthesis   process by which plants make food using light energy from the Sun

## Food chains

Animals cannot make their own food like plants do. They need to eat plants or other animals to get energy. For example, rabbits eat plants, and foxes eat rabbits. The way the energy is passed along from plants to animals is called a **food chain**.

## Food webs

Each food chain starts with a plant because plants get their energy from the Sun. Each plant is eaten by many different animals, and most animals live off different kinds of food. The many different food chains in an area can be linked together to make a **food web**.

### Part of the chain

Many animals live off plants that get their energy from the Sun. The zebra below is being chased by a lion. If the lion catches and eats the zebra, the energy from the Sun will have passed along the food chain to the lion.

food chain   chain of living things linked by what they eat

## Ecosystems

Scientists are interested to see how **energy** flows through the **food chains** and **food webs** in an **ecosystem.** They do this by counting the number of plants and animals in an area, and also by measuring their weight.

## Pyramids of numbers

The number of living things in a food chain can be shown in a bar graph called a pyramid of numbers. Each bar represents the number of a type of plant or animal. The bar on the bottom is always the plant at the start of the food chain.

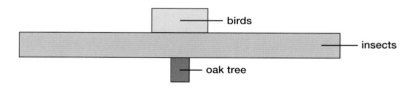

The pyramid of numbers above is for the food chain *oak tree → insect → bird.* One oak tree provides food for lots of insects, but the insects feed only a small number of birds.

### Food chain

This picture (below) shows the members of the food chain: *oak tree→insect→bird.*

ecosystem    group of animals and plants and the place they live in

## Pyramids of biomass

It is possible to draw another kind of pyramid that shows the mass, also called weight, of living things in a food chain. These are called pyramids of **biomass**.

The pyramid of biomass for the *oak tree → insect → bird* food chain looks very different from the pyramid of numbers. Although there is only one oak tree, it has a very large mass. Birds are heavier than insects, but there are fewer of them, so their total biomass is smaller.

birds

insects

oak tree

**Samples**
This diver (left) is collecting some coral in order to weigh it. From this information, he will be able to make a pyramid of biomass.

**biomass**   total mass of living things at each level in a food chain

## Burning biomass

**Biomass fuel** is a useful form of **renewable energy**. This is material from living things that can be used as fuel. The most common biomass fuel is wood from trees.

## Burning wood

We have seen how plants use the Sun's energy to grow. Trees store **chemical energy** in their trunks and branches. When a tree is cut down and the wood is burned, the chemical energy is changed into heat and light energy.

### Fast-growing trees

Poplars and willows (above) are often grown for biomass fuel. The wood grows quickly and can be cut for firewood every three years.

biomass fuel    material from living things, used as a renewable energy resource

## Nonpolluting

Burning biomass fuel is not a danger to the **atmosphere** in the same way that **fossil fuels** are. This is because as the trees are growing they take carbon dioxide out of the atmosphere. When the wood is burned, it puts back the same amount of carbon dioxide. The balance of the gas in the atmosphere has not changed.

### Wood chip power stations

Small pieces of wood, called wood chips, burn much better than large logs. Some **power stations** such as the one in the United States (below), now use wood chips.

atmosphere   layer of gases that surround Earth

25

▲ In Brazil, ethanol is mixed with gasoline to make a fuel called gasohol (above).

## Other biomass fuels

Material from living things can be made into liquid **biomass fuels**, such as ethanol. They can also be made into gases such as methane. These fuels are often more useful than wood because they are a more concentrated source of **energy**.

## Ethanol

Ethanol is a clear, colorless liquid that burns very easily. It makes a good fuel. It is made by **fermenting** the sugars in sugarcane into alcohol. Because new sugarcane can always be grown, ethanol is a **renewable energy resource**.

## Biodiesel

The seeds from rapeseed, or canola (right), crops are rich in oil and can be made into a liquid fuel called biodiesel.

ferment   when yeast converts sugars in plant material into carbon dioxide and alcohol

## Benefits of biomass energy

- It is a renewable resource and will never run out.
- It does not add to **global warming**.

## Problems of biomass energy

- Wood takes up a lot of space. It makes lots of smoke and ash when it burns.
- Wood is more difficult to burn than **fossil fuels**.
- Forests are damaged if new trees are not replanted.
- Biomass crops cover huge areas of land. These could be used to grow food instead of making biomass fuel.

### Biogas

Animal manure gives off a gas called methane as it rots. This "biogas" can be collected and used for cooking and can even run small **power stations**. The picture below shows a small biogas collector in India.

**global warming**   extra warming of Earth caused by an increased greenhouse effect

# Wind Energy

Wind is also a **renewable energy resource**. The **kinetic energy** in wind can be used to drive all sorts of machines. It can also be turned into electrical energy.

## Where does the wind come from?

The Sun warms up the land. The warm land heats the air above it, and the warmed air starts to rise. In other parts of the world, air is cooling down and sinking. The cool air moves across the land to take the place of the rising warm air. This movement of air across the land is called wind.

▲ The huge amount of energy in **hurricane** force winds can rip up trees, damage buildings, and throw cars around (above).

### Sailing ships

Sailing ships have used the energy in the wind to transport goods around the world for centuries.

**Word Store**   hurricane   very powerful storm with high winds

## A renewable energy resource

The energy from the wind comes from the Sun's heat energy. As long as the Sun keeps shining and the winds keep blowing, we will be able to use the energy from the wind.

### Windsurfing
Windsurfers use kinetic energy from the wind to speed along the surface of the sea (left).

## Windmills

Windmills use the **kinetic energy** in the wind to turn machinery. The sails on a windmill are split into two or more **blades**. These are twisted or tilted slightly to make sure they catch the wind. Windmills work best when they face the wind.

### *Pumping water*

Water can be pumped up from underground using windmills. Farms in dry areas often use steel wind pumps (above) to bring water to the surface.

## Early windmills

The very first windmills were used to turn the machinery that ground wheat into flour. This is called milling. This is how they got the name "windmill." Since then, windmills have been used for many different tasks.

## Reclaiming land

In the Netherlands, much land that was once under the sea has been **reclaimed**. This was done by building barriers behind the seashore and then pumping the sea water out. The water was carried away in canals leaving dry land behind. Windmills connected to water pumps were used to do this. Once they were built, the windmills could be kept running very cheaply.

◀ ▼ Old windmills like these were used for pumping water to drain land or for milling grain to make flour.

**Savonius wind turbine**

The Savonius wind **turbine** (above) was invented in Finland in the 1920s. It looked very different from other windmills. It was made of metal and had S-shaped blades, which meant it always worked whatever the direction of the wind.

reclaim   make land useful again

## Electricity from the wind

Modern windmills are called wind **turbines**. The **energy** from wind turbines is used to turn **generators** to make electricity. Modern wind turbines are much more **efficient** than old windmills. They turn much more of the wind's energy into useful energy.

## Made to go faster

Modern windmills need to be able to spin very quickly. They have two or three thin **blades** that look like airplane propellers. These are fixed to the top of tall towers. Because the blades are on towers, the land below can still be used for farming.

### Wind farms

In places where there is a lot of wind, many wind turbines are built together to make a wind farm. Some people do not like living near wind farms as they can be quite noisy.

▶ This modern wind turbine will work whichever way the wind is blowing from.

turbine   machinery that is turned by moving air, water, or steam

## Benefits of wind power

- Wind turbines do not need fuel to run them.
- They do not make any **pollution**.
- Once the wind turbines have been built, their **running costs** are low.
- Turbines need replacing only every 25 years.

## Problems with wind power

- Wind turbines work only on windy days.
- They must be shut down if the wind is blowing too hard.
- Not all areas are windy enough for **wind farms**.
- People do not like wind farms because they spoil the view of the countryside and are noisy.

### Offshore wind farms

It is possible to build wind farms out at sea. These are called **offshore** wind farms. Offshore wind farms have all the benefits of wind power but fewer problems. However, they are much more expensive to build in the first place. This is an offshore wind turbine (left). The base sits on the seabed.

offshore   built out at sea

# Energy from Moving Water

The **kinetic energy** in moving water can be used to drive all sorts of machinery, such as electricity **generators**.

## The water cycle

Water **evaporates** from seas, lakes, and rivers to form a gas called **water vapor**. Water vapor rises into the sky, where it cools and **condenses** into water droplets. These collect together and fall to Earth as rain. Rain flows into rivers and then back to the sea. This is called the water cycle.

▲ Rivers will always flow, so they are a good source of **renewable** energy.

## The water cycle

The picture, right, shows the water cycle. Heat energy from the Sun keeps the cycle going.

condensation

evaporation

rain, snow, or hail

heated by the Sun

water runs off land into oceans

evaporate   change from a liquid to a gas

## Energy from rivers

As long as it keeps on raining, rivers will flow and the **energy** in them can be used.

Watermills are built next to rivers. A waterwheel is built on the side of the mill. The waterwheel has **blades** that catch the water and make the wheel turn. It turns slowly but is very powerful. Waterwheels often drive machinery for grinding wheat or pumping water. In the old days, many towns were built near rivers so waterwheels could be used.

### Mill ponds

If there is no rain and no water in the rivers, a waterwheel (below) cannot turn. To get around this problem, watermills had mill ponds that stored water. When the river was dry, water could be let out of the pond to turn the waterwheel.

## Hydroelectric power

Water always flows from high places to low places. **Hydroelectric power** (HEP) stations are able to change the **kinetic energy** in the moving water into electrical **energy**.

In most HEP stations, a **dam** is built across a river, making a lake. The water is let out of the lake through pipes. Inside the pipes are **turbines** that turn electricity **generators**. The farther water falls, and the faster it flows, the more kinetic energy it has. This is why HEP stations are usually built in hilly areas with lots of rain.

### The Dinorwig power station

The Dinorwig HEP station in Wales, in the United Kingdom (above) makes electricity during the day. At night, cheap electricity is used to pump water back to the lake ready to use again the next day.

dam    barrier built across a river to block it so that water can be stored

## Hoover Dam

Hoover Dam was built on the Colorado River in the southwest United States in the 1930s. Its turbines can make all the electricity needed by a city of 750,000 people. During busy times, enough water runs through the turbines to fill fifteen swimming pools every second.

## Niagara Falls

Niagara Falls (below) is part of a huge hydroelectric power project. Two HEP stations take water out of the river before the falls.

### Lake Mead

This is Hoover Dam (below). The **reservoir** behind the dam is called Lake Mead. It has an area of 229 square miles (593 square kilometers).

generator    equipment used to make electricity

## Tidal power

Tidal power uses the power of a different type of moving water to make electricity. This is the energy stored in sea water, which moves with the tides each day.

The Moon's **gravity** pulls the water in Earth's seas toward it. This makes the sea level rise wherever Earth is facing the Moon. This makes a high tide. Everywhere else, the sea level goes down, making a low tide. As Earth turns, high tides and low tides happen in different places on Earth through the day and night.

### Biggest barrage

The world's biggest tidal barrage is at La Rance in France (below). It is almost half a mile (750 meters) long. It makes as much electricity as a small power station. It can power 20,000 homes.

gravity   force that makes things fall downward

## Tidal barrages

To use the **kinetic energy** in tidal water, a long dam called a **barrage** is built. Pipes inside the barrage let sea water in and out. The moving water turns **turbines** inside the pipes. The turbines turn the electricity **generators**.

Some tidal barrages make electricity only as the tide goes out. Others, like the one at La Rance in France (see the picture at the left), make electricity as the tide comes in as well.

### Tidal bores

In some rivers, a strange thing happens when the tide comes in. The sea pushes the river water back upstream, making a powerful wave called a tidal bore. Tidal bores can travel a few miles (several kilometers) inland. It is even possible to surf on them (below).

**barrage**   long dam built across a bay or river mouth

## Wave power

Moving waves have a lot of **kinetic energy**. We can use the energy in the waves to make electricity.

## Up and down

When ocean waves reach the beach, they curl over and break. But in deeper water, the water just rises up-and-down. This movement is used by wave machines. Scientists are still trying to find the best way to trap energy from waves.

### Salter's Duck

"Floaters" are wave machines that bob up and down on the surface of the sea. As they do this, they change the energy in the water into energy that turns an electricity **generator**. The Salter's Duck (below) is one design of floater.

▲ Surfers use the kinetic energy in waves to surf along at great speeds.

## Benefits of water-powered devices

- They do not need fuel to run them.
- They do not make any **pollution**.
- They are cheap to run.
- They do not often break.
- **Dams** and tidal **barrages** can also be used as bridges.

## Problems with water power

- Dams and lakes can destroy homes and wildlife.
- Building costs are very high.
- Electricity is made a long way from where it is needed, so it has to be transported using a lot of wires.
- Mud builds up behind dams, making them less useful.

### Sitters

"Sitters" are wave machines that are fixed in one place. This is the Limpet, a wave machine built on the Scottish island of Islay. It makes enough electricity for 300 houses.

dam   barrier built across a river to block it so that water can be stored

# What Next?

We know that, whatever we do, **fossil fuels** will run out one day. However, as long as light and heat **energy** from the Sun reach Earth, **renewable energy resources** will never run out. In the future, all the world's energy needs will have to come from renewable resources.

## Big projects

Many renewable energy projects are very big. Some of the projects, such as building **dams** and tidal **barrages** will change the **environment**. Are these big projects a good idea for the future?

### Make your own

The solar cells on this office building make all the electricity the building needs during the day. It would be good if more houses and businesses could use solar power to make the electricity they use themselves.

renewable    will not run out and can be replaced

## Small designs

There are many ways in which small-scale designs can be built to use renewable energy resources. **Solar** panels can easily be attached to roofs to heat water. Small wind **turbines** and solar cells can be built into the walls and roofs of buildings to make electricity. Many small pieces of equipment that can be powered by renewable energy resources are now being invented.

In the future, we are likely to see an interesting and exciting mix of renewable energy resources being used to power our world.

### Micro-HEP stations

This is a micro-**hydroelectric power station** in Scotland (below). It uses the water in a small river to provide electricity for a small village. The water is returned to the river downstream so the environment is not damaged in any way.

# Find Out More

## Organizations

### US Department of Energy

**Energy Efficiency and Renewable Energy**
This site gives a useful overview of the renewable energy technologies available today. Learn how to buy clean electricity, get energy from trash, and how to make your house more energy efficient.

Contact them at the following address:

Energy Efficiency and
Renewable Energy
Mail Stop EE-1
Department of
Energy
Washington, DC
20585
(202) 586-9220

## Books

Parker, Steve. *Solar Power (Science Files: Energy)*. Milwaukee: Gareth Stevens, 2004.

Saunders, Nigel, and Steven Chapman. *Fossil Fuel (Energy Essentials)*. Chicago: Raintree, 2005.

Sneddon, Robert. *Energy Alternatives (Essential Energy)*. Chicago: Heinemann Library, 2001.

## World Wide Web

To find out more about renewable energy, you can search the Internet using keywords like these:

- "renewable energy"
- "alternative energy"
- biodiesel +biomass
- "tidal power"
- "wave power"

You can find your own keywords by using words from this book. The search tips opposite will help you find the most useful web sites.

## Search tips

There are billions of pages on the Internet. It can be difficult to find exactly what you are looking for. These tips will help you find useful web sites more quickly:

- Know what you want to find out about.
- Use simple keywords.
- Use two to six keywords in a search.
- Only use names of people, places, or things.
- Put double quote marks around words that go together, for example "wave power"

## Where to search

### Search engine

A search engine looks through millions of web site pages. It lists all the sites that match the words in the search box. You will find that the best matches are at the top of the list, on the first page.

### Search directory

A person instead of a computer has sorted a search directory. You can search by keyword or subject and browse through the different sites. It is like looking through books on a library shelf.

# Glossary

**absorb** take in

**acid rain** rain that contains substances that damage buildings and living things

**atmosphere** layer of gases that surrounds Earth

**barrage** long dam built across a bay or river mouth

**biomass** total mass of living things at each level in a food chain

**biomass fuel** material from living things, used as a renewable energy resource

**blade** spinning arm on a windmill or turbine

**chemical energy** stored energy in chemicals

**condense** change from a gas to a liquid

**contract** become smaller and fill less space

**dam** barrier built across a river to block it so that water can be stored

**ecosystem** group of animals and plants and the place they live in

**efficient** good at doing a job without wasting energy

**energy** being able to do work. Light, heat, and electricity are types of energy.

**energy resource** source or store of energy, such as hydroelectric power and coal

**environment** the world around us

**evaporate** change from a liquid to a gas

**expand** get bigger

**ferment** when yeast converts sugars in

plant material into carbon dioxide and alcohol

**focus** concentrate onto one spot

**food chain** chain of living things linked by what they eat

**food web** two or more food chains joined together

**fossil fuel** fuel made from the remains of fossilized plants or animals

**fossilized** turned into stone

**generator** machine used to make electricity

**global warming** extra warming of Earth caused by an increased greenhouse effect

**gravity** force that makes objects fall downward

**greenhouse effect** keeping the atmosphere warm by trapping heat

**hurricane** very powerful storm, with high winds

**hydroelectric power** electricity made using the energy in moving water

**insulated** covered in material that reduces heat loss

**kinetic energy** energy of moving things

**mineral** substance needed by plants and animals to keep them healthy

**nonrenewable** something that will run out one day and cannot be replaced

**offshore** built out at sea

**passive** something that happens with no machinery or extra energy needed

**photosynthesis** process by which plants make food using light energy from the Sun

**pollution** harmful substances in the air, in the water, or on land

**power station** place where electricity is generated

**reclaim** make land useful again

**reflect** shine back light

**renewable** will not run out and can be replaced

**reservoir** large lake behind a dam, used for storing water

**running cost** cost of keeping equipment working

**satellite** something that goes around a planet

**smog** mixture of smoke and fog

**solar** anything to do with the Sun

**turbine** machinery that is turned by moving air, water, or steam

**water vapor** water in gas form

**wind farm** lots of wind turbines in one place

# Index